Peaceful Piggy Yoga

Kerry Lee MacLean

FICTION READALONG
AV² BY WEIGL™
ADDED VALUE • AUDIO VISUAL

Go to **www.av2books.com**, and enter this book's unique code.

BOOK CODE

T829764

AV² by Weigl brings you media enhanced books that support active learning.

First Published by

ALBERT WHITMAN & COMPANY
Publishing children's books since 1919

Your AV² Media Enhanced book gives you a fiction readalong online. Log on to www.av2books.com and enter the unique book code from this page to use your readalong.

AV² Readalong Navigation

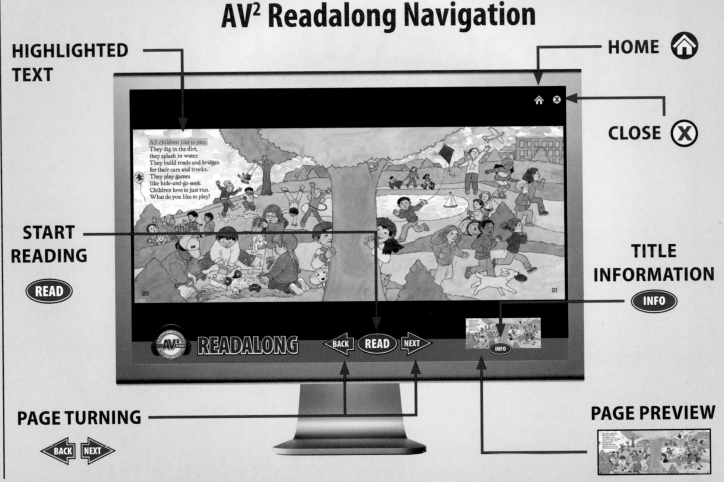

HIGHLIGHTED TEXT

HOME

CLOSE

START READING

TITLE INFORMATION

PAGE TURNING

PAGE PREVIEW

Published by AV² by Weigl
350 5th Avenue, 59th Floor New York, NY 10118
Website: www.av2books.com   www.weigl.com

Printed in the United States of America in North Mankato, Minnesota
1 2 3 4 5 6 7 8 9 0   17 16 15 14 13

052013
WEP250413

Library of Congress Control Number: 2013939939

ISBN 978-1-62127-886-3 (hardcover)
ISBN 978-1-48961-457-5 (single-user eBook)
ISBN 978-1-48961-458-2 (multi-user eBook)

Text and illustrations copyright ©2008 by Kerry Lee MacLean.
Published in 2008 by Albert Whitman & Company.

∙ ⌇∘ How to Use This Book ∙∘⌇ ∘

Yoga is a series of gentle stretches that bring joy and relaxation. You should never stretch muscles to the point of pain, but just enough to feel a nice pull. Try to hold each pose for at least three deep breaths. The Peaceful Piggy yoga series is safe for piggies of all ages. It can be done at home as a nice way to spend time with parents, brothers, and sisters; at school in the classroom (before a test or just to calm and quiet everyone); and just about anywhere with your friends. Regular practice teaches piggies that caring for their minds and bodies feels good—and it can even be fun!

Tree Pose

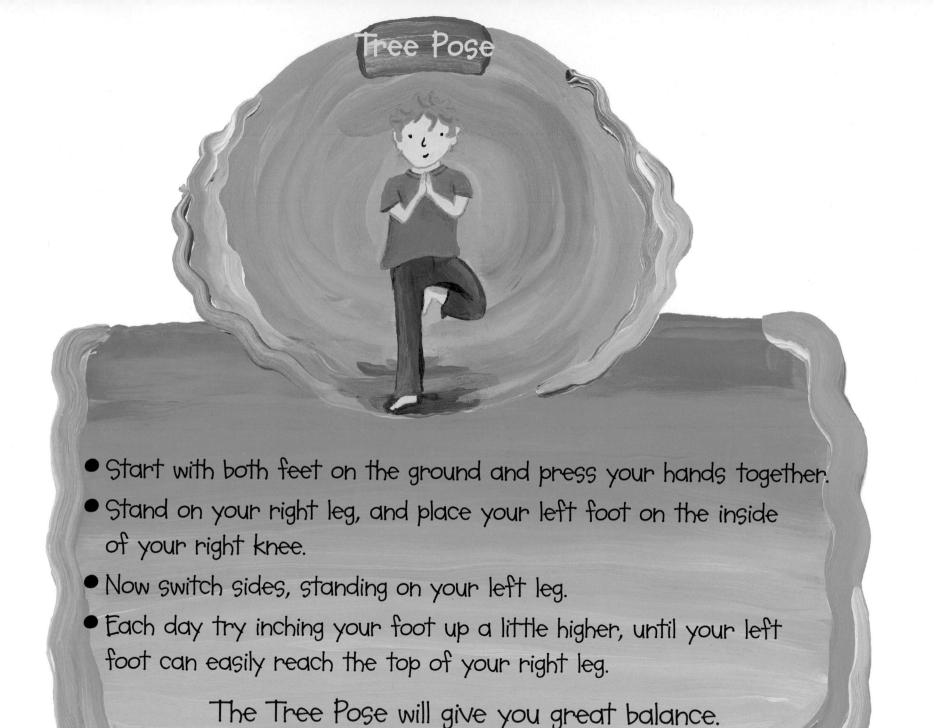

- Start with both feet on the ground and press your hands together.
- Stand on your right leg, and place your left foot on the inside of your right knee.
- Now switch sides, standing on your left leg.
- Each day try inching your foot up a little higher, until your left foot can easily reach the top of your right leg.

The Tree Pose will give you great balance.

Candlestick

- To start, lie on your back with your knees bent.
- Lift your legs up toward the ceiling and straighten them.
- Move your arms to hold your lower back firmly with your hands.
- Be sure to support most of your weight on your shoulders—not your neck!
- Try to keep your legs as straight as a candlestick.

This stretches your back.
It's good for the heart, too!

Moms and dads do it for **peace of mind.**

Full Lotus

- Start by sitting cross-legged.
- Gently pull each foot up onto the opposite thigh. (If this is too hard, try the Half Lotus on page 23.)
- Make sure your back is straight and your chest is open so you can breathe better.
- Keep your eyes open, looking at the ground in front of you.
- Don't think too much; just rest your mind by feeling your breath go in and out, in and out. Count up to ten breaths.

This pose will help you feel a peaceful place inside.

Football players do yoga to get **stronger.**

Gate Pose

- Kneel on your right knee with the left leg stretched out to the side.
- Make sure your left leg is slightly bent.
- Your left heel should be in line with your right knee.
- Put your left hand on your left ankle.
- Stretch your right arm over your head until you feel a gentle pull.
- Repeat on the other side.

This pose opens your rib cage so you can breathe more deeply.

Ballerinas do yoga for better **balance.**

Hand-Toe Pose

- Start in the Tree Pose position (page 5).
- Put your left hand on hip—or on the back of a chair, if you need help with balance.
- Grab your right ankle with your right hand.
- Slowly pull your leg up in front of you, then swing it out to the side.
- It may take some practice before you can extend your leg all the way.
- Repeat on the other side.

This pose gives you excellent balance and makes
your stomach strong.

Warrior Pose

- Take a big step to the side with your left foot.
- Turn your left foot so that your toes are facing left. Turn your right foot slightly to the left.
- Gently bend your left knee. Keep your right leg straight.
- Make sure your knee doesn't bend too far forward. It should stay directly over your ankle.
- Keep your torso upright and your arms parallel to the ground.
- Repeat on the other side.

This pose makes your legs strong!

Cowboys do yoga after a **hard day** in the saddle.

Seated Twist

- Sit with your left knee bent and your right leg extended.
- Put your left hand on the floor behind your back.
- Bring your right elbow over and around your left knee.
- If you can, try twisting further until you can clasp both hands behind your back—but don't overdo it!
- Hold for one to five breaths.

This pose stretches your whole torso, back and front.

Babies do yoga without even **knowing** it!

18

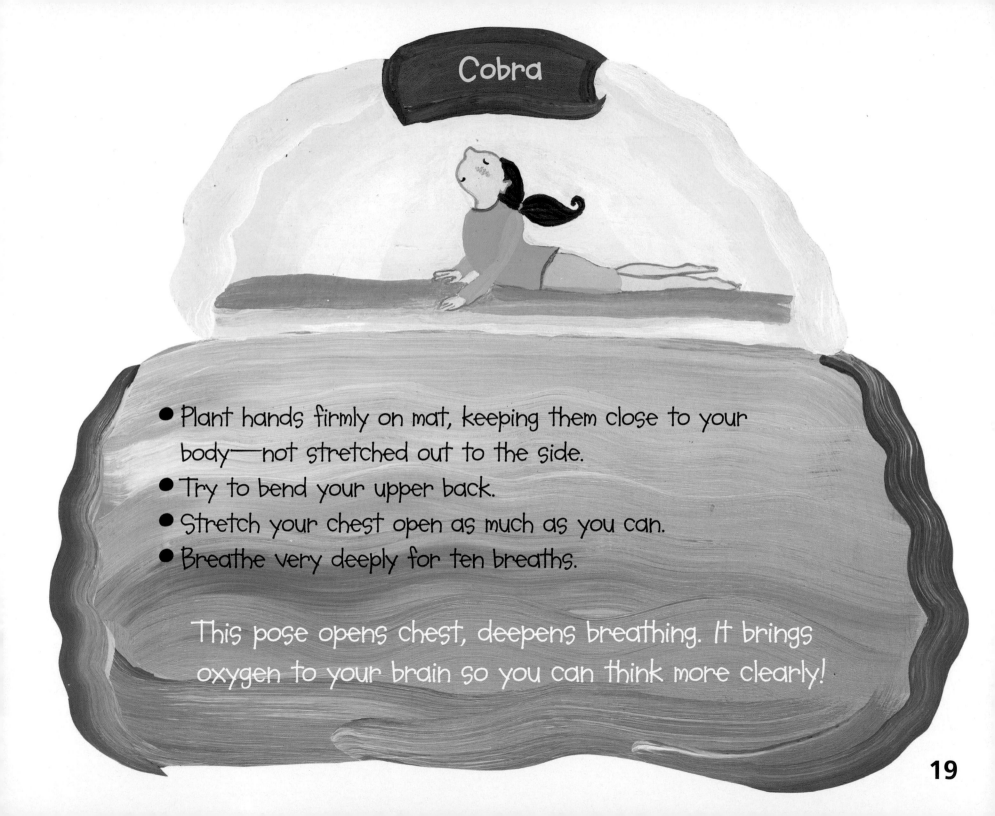

Cobra

- Plant hands firmly on mat, keeping them close to your body—not stretched out to the side.
- Try to bend your upper back.
- Stretch your chest open as much as you can.
- Breathe very deeply for ten breaths.

This pose opens chest, deepens breathing. It brings oxygen to your brain so you can think more clearly!

You can do yoga anytime,
anywhere, any place!

Lord of the Dance

- Start by balancing on your left foot. Bend your right leg backward, lifting the right foot up.
- Now reach back and grab your right foot with your right hand.
- Slowly extend your left arm. Try to gently lift your right leg a little higher.
- Repeat on the other side.
- If you have trouble balancing, try facing a wall. You can support yourself against the wall with your forward hand.

Stretches spine and improves balance.

21

Try yoga at school to get **calm** and **clear** before a spelling test.

Half Lotus

- Sit cross-legged.
- Gently stretch one foot up onto the opposite thigh. Leave the other foot on the ground.
- A straight back and open chest make room for lots of breath.
- Rest open eyes on the ground before you.
- Angry thoughts? Let them go. Happy thoughts? Let them go. Just focus on the breath going in and out, in and out.

This pose is one-half the strain
of the Full Lotus.

And at bedtime— when you're too **rootin' tootin'** riled up to go to sleep . . .

the Corpse Pose will help you **calm down.**

Corpse Pose

- Lay flat on your back.
- Close your eyes.
- Rest your arms a couple of inches out from your body.
  They should be straight but relaxed with palms up.
- No snoring!

This posture is extremely calming. Sweet dreams!

Daily yoga helps piggies **concentrate better** . . .

climb higher than ever **before** . . .

which means **peaceful piggies** feel

The Peaceful Piggy Yoga Series

Try this series of postures!

Tree Pose
Page 5

Candlestick
Page 7

Warrior Pose
Page 15

Seated Twist
Page 17

Cobra
Page 19

Full Lotus
Page 9

Gate Pose
Page 11

Hand-Toe Pose
Page 13

Lord of the Dance
Page 21

Half Lotus
Page 23

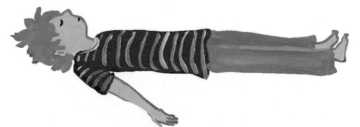

Corpse Pose
Page 25

To Gregory Michael MacLean, a mad yogi at heart,
and to my peaceful piggy yogin and yogini friends everywhere!—K.M.